5 Days to a Perfect Night's Sleep for Your Child

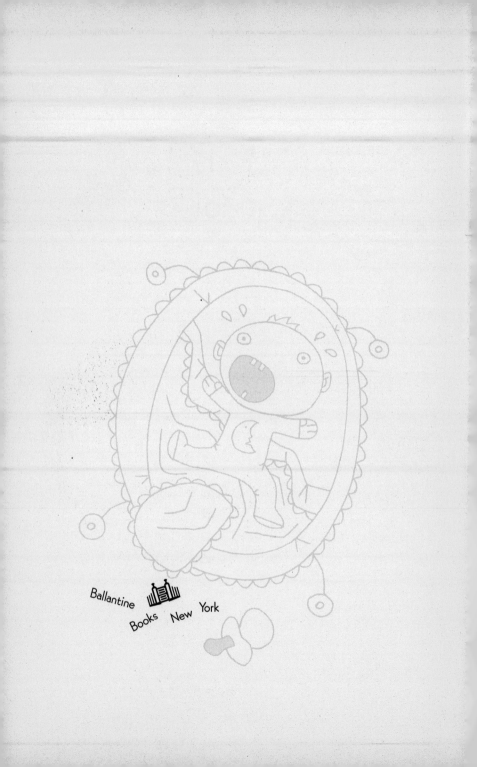

Ballantine Books   New York

5 Days to a Perfect Night's Sleep for Your Child

The Secrets to Making Bedtime a Dream

Eduard Estivill, M.D.

Translated from the Spanish by
Mara Faye Lethem

Revised by
Rachel Anderson

No book can replace the diagnostic expertise and medical advice of a
trusted physician. Please be certain to consult with your doctor before
making any decisions that affect the health of you or your child,
particularly if either of you suffers from any medical condition or have
any symptoms that may require treatment.

A 2008 Ballantine Books Trade Paperback Original

English translation copyright © 2008 by Mara Faye Lethem

Illustrations copyright © 2002 by Clara Roca

Published in the United States by Ballantine Books,
an imprint of The Random House Publishing Group,
a division of Random House, Inc., New York.

BALLANTINE and colophon are registered
trademarks of Random House, Inc.

Originally published in Spain as *Método Estivill, Guía rápida*
by Plaza & Janés, an imprint of Random House
Mondadori, S. A., Barcelona, in 2002.

Copyright © 2002 by Eduard Estivill
Illustrations copyright © 2002 by Clara Roca

Copyright © 2002 by Random House Mondadori, S. A.

ISBN 978-0-345-50180-6

Printed in the United States of America

www.ballantinebooks.com

2 4 6 8 9 7 5 3 1

Book design by Simon M. Sullivan

To my friends, the parents; to my colleagues, the pediatricians;
and to my beloved kids, who will someday be parents themselves.

CONTENTS

INTRODUCTION

Twenty years ago, I began studying childhood insomnia. Since then, I have personally treated more than three thousand children with sleep disorders and written a book that parents have affectionately dubbed *The Estivill Method*. Throughout this time, my method has taught tens of thousands of kids in more than twenty countries how to sleep.

Here, I'll guide you through my method. Essentially a series of steps that, if used correctly, promise to end all the sleepless nights, this book is a store of knowledge based on scientific research, carefully organized with the goal of teaching you how to help your children achieve proper sleep habits.

This method is not meant to be preachy and in no way claims to be the only possible solution. What's important about this guide is that it is easily applicable to those of you who choose to use it.

As a parent, you know better than anyone that teaching your child to sleep isn't easy. But it's definitely not impossible, even though it may have felt that way on more than one desperate occasion. From my clinical experience (those three thousand small patients) and the comments I've gotten from parents and pediatricians who have put my method into practice, I can assure you of a 96 percent success rate if the rules mapped out in this book are strictly applied. And by *strictly*, I mean rigorously, not harshly. Just follow this method to the letter and it will work. I promise.

Chapter 1
My Child Doesn't Sleep Well

WORDS OF ADVICE

Before you start, please read the following recommendations carefully.

- First of all, you need to be convinced that this method will work for you. In order to teach a child healthy sleep habits, *you*, the parent, grandparent, babysitter, or caretaker, are the key player in the process. And your confidence in this method is essential to your success! If you trust the method completely, you will project your confidence to your child and will see quick and tangible results. You will be faced with new situations, and—trust me—many of them will be extremely trying, especially at 4 AM. This is why all the caretakers must work together, drawing from the same set of standards and following the same rules.

- Make sure that your child doesn't have medical ailments when you begin treatment. Methodically rule out any type of illness that may be causing your child to sleep poorly, the most common of which are ear infections, lactose intolerance, gastric reflux, and, occasionally, psychological or psychiatric problems. Consult your pediatrician to help you with this.

- Recognize that all kids can learn to sleep well even though each child is different and has a unique personality. Some kids catch on quicker than others. Some do as they're told. Others are more stubborn. Some children are calm and some, more active. From the minute your child is born, you, as a parent, start to see these different personality traits. And of course

All caregivers should be involved in the treatment and should understand the technique of teaching a habit.

they're important, but they should never be used as an excuse to justify insomnia. Teaching your baby to sleep simply means teaching her correct sleep behavior! We learn to sleep, just as we learn to eat, read, and go to the bathroom. Sure, there are active kids who can barely sit still, so it's tough imagining them reading a story quietly to themselves. But they will figure it out, sooner or later.

- Remember that your child needs you. You, the parents and caretakers, are the ones who will teach her how to sleep on her own; she can't learn this alone. My method offers you all the tools you need. First I'll explain what good sleep behavior involves; then I'll help you teach this to your child. So stop feeling powerless! There's no reason to feel guilty: *No one has ever explained to you how a child learns to sleep.* All you need is someone to help guide you!

- After so many nights of collective insomnia, you are probably feeling exhausted, irritable, and nervous, but remember that your child is suffering, too. Sleep is an important part of everyone's life, and children who sleep poorly are usually crankier and more dependent on their caregivers than kids who sleep well. Once they've completed my method, many parents feel that they are looking at a whole different child. They say things like, "She's calmer, she's in a good mood, she plays by herself more often, and she's even nicer." But this isn't true. Your baby was born nice and was simply suffering from sleep deprivation.

WHY IS IT IMPORTANT FOR MY CHILD TO SLEEP WELL?

One simple reason: Nobody can live without sleep, not even animals. During sleep, a child's brain grows and matures more rapidly than it does during daylight hours. Additionally, the body creates everything it will use throughout the next day, which is why a child who doesn't sleep well at night is cranky, nervous, tired, and drowsy in the morning.

WHY DOESN'T MY KID SLEEP WELL?

Before jumping into the method, let's take an inside look at the physiological aspects of sleep. To begin, let's define what a biological rhythm is and how long it lasts.

Biological Rhythms

A *biological rhythm* is the systematic repetition of a pattern that takes place in the body, such as the pattern of sleep and

CONSEQUENCES OF SLEEP DEPRIVATION

On Nursing Babies and Toddlers

- Irritability, crankiness
- Frequent crying
- Dependence on their caregivers; inability to be on their own

On School-Aged Kids

- Problems with schoolwork
- Insecurity and shyness
- Attitude problems

On Parents

- Tiredness
- Insecurity
- Guilt
- Mutual blame
- Drastic changes in a couple's relationship
- Frustration with the situation
- Feelings of failure or helplessness
- Aggressive behavior

wakefulness. Infants repeat a specific biological cycle every three to four hours, which includes such activities as waking up, eating, being bathed, and sleeping. This kind of cycle is called an *ultradian rhythm*.

Adults follow a circadian rhythm. The word *circadian* comes from the Latin *circa*, meaning "about" or "approximately," and *diem* meaning "day." The adult pattern of sleep

SLEEP PATTERNS OF NEWBORNS IN THE FIRST MONTH

The Ultradian Rhythm of Three to Four Hours

and wakefulness is repeated (approximately) every twenty-four hours.

When Does This Biological Rhythm Change?

Once babies are three or four months old, they begin to progressively lengthen their biological rhythm as they adapt

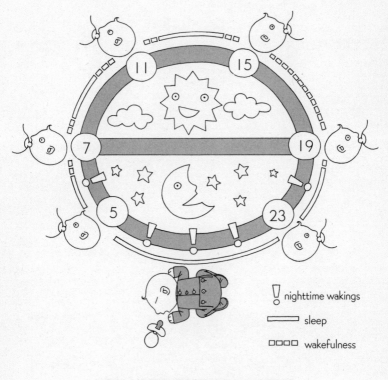

! nighttime wakings

▭ sleep

▱▱▱▱ wakefulness

SLEEP PATTERNS BETWEEN THE FIRST
AND FOURTH MONTHS

from the three- to four-hour ultradian rhythm to the adult twenty-four-hour cycle. At this age, babies start to sleep six hours in a row—a huge gift to parents!

Once a baby is six months old, she should sleep for twelve hours straight with two or three short (one-hour) naps during the day—one after breakfast, another after lunch, and the last one, which is optional and shorter, after a snack.

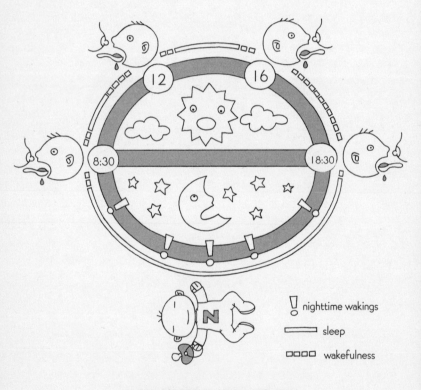

nighttime wakings

sleep

wakefulness

SLEEP PATTERNS AT SIX MONTHS
TWENTY-FOUR-HOUR CIRCADIAN RHYTHM

How Does This Change Happen?

This change comes about thanks to a group of cells in the human brain* that work like a clock. The goal of this "clock" is to adjust a person's needs to the twenty-four-hour biological rhythm.

Think of this as an old kind of clock that needs to be wound. Seventy percent of newborns manage to "set" their clocks with a few routines or some simple encouragement from their parents, such as being picked up, put in a crib, told good night, rocked a bit, or sung a lullaby.

Not all children set their own clocks, however. The other 30 percent of babies *can* sleep just as well as those in the first group—they simply need a bit more "winding." It is very easy to readjust a sleep cycle, but it has to be done as soon as possible. My experience shows that the earlier you start to correct bad sleep habits, the easier they are to solve. So let's get started!

How Can You Wind the Sleep Clock?

You can set your baby's clock by exposing her to certain external stimuli.

- *Reinforce the contrast between* light (day) and dark (night); and the contrast between noise (day) and silence (night). In this way, you promote the idea that

---

*The medical term is *the suprachiasmatic nucleus of the hypothalamus*.

light and noise are part of daytime wakefulness, while darkness and silence are associated with nighttime and sleeping. During the day, never create an artificial environment. Don't lower the shades or tiptoe around while your baby is napping. Just act normally!

- *Use meals as a cue* to announce your child's next nap or nighttime sleep.

- *Teach sleep habits.* Show your baby how to fall asleep on her own, without anyone's help. Don't worry: I'll explain this more in the next section!

CLINICAL CHARACTERISTICS OF INFANT INSOMNIA (CAUSED BY INCORRECT SLEEP HABITS)

If your child doesn't manage to change her biological rhythm and doesn't learn to sleep correctly, she'll suffer what is clinically called *infant insomnia*. The characteristics of this disorder are:

- Difficulty falling asleep alone.

- Waking up often at night.

- Sleeping lightly (waking up at the slightest noise).

- Sleeping fewer hours than normal for children of the same age.

If your child exhibits the above behavior, don't be alarmed! She is perfectly normal both physically and psychologically. She just hasn't learned how to sleep properly—a problem you are about to solve.

SUMMARY

My Child Doesn't Sleep Well:
Sleep Physiology and the Biological Clock

- Newborns have an ultradian biological rhythm that lasts between three and four hours. During this period, they wake up, are bathed, eat, sleep, and repeat the process.

- At about six months of age, babies adapt to a circadian rhythm, which means that the systematic sequence of activities repeats itself every twenty-four hours. At night, they should sleep between eleven and twelve hours straight (in addition to their daytime naps).

Seventy percent of children adjust to this cycle without any problems thanks to a group of cells in the human brain that work like a clock.

The other 30 percent need external stimuli to help them "wind" their clock:

- Reinforce the contrast between light (day) and darkness (night); between noise (day) and silence (night).

- Use meals to cue bedtime.

- Understand that they can and will fall asleep on their own.

Chapter 2
What Are Good Sleep Habits?

All of us, at some point, have dreamed of returning to childhood: that glorious stage of life when we didn't have to punch in at eight o'clock in the morning or worry about leaky faucets. During the early years of life, our only obligations are eating and sleeping. Sounds pretty good!

Still, you can be sure that even these were not such simple tasks, at least not at first. We all had to learn to do them correctly; if nobody had ever taught us to use a fork and spoon, we might still be mopping up our spaghetti sauce with our fingers. And it might never have occurred to us that a balanced diet can involve more than chocolate!

From this, we can reach two crucial conclusions. First, eating is not the same as eating well, and—in much the same way—*sleeping is not the same as sleeping well*. Clearly, your baby sleeps at some point during the day—he couldn't live if he didn't. However, it's another thing altogether to sleep correctly. So how can you know if your child is sleeping well?

Very simply. If you can answer yes to the following questions, then there is no problem:

- Does he go to sleep happily and without crying?

- Does he fall asleep on his own?

- Does he sleep in his crib with the lights turned off?

- Does he sleep for eleven or twelve hours straight? (Although some children need a bit less, this is the average.)

Second, *sleeping, just like eating, is learned.* Sleep is a habit and, as such, must be taught.

HOW IS A HABIT FORMED?

Let's use the food example to understand how you teach a child a habit:

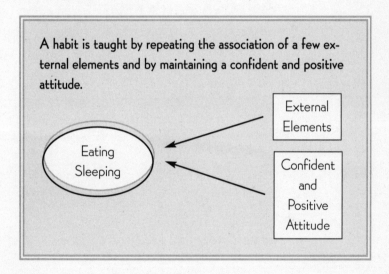

A habit is taught by repeating the association of a few external elements and by maintaining a confident and positive attitude.

Eating
Sleeping

External Elements

Confident and Positive Attitude

The Association of External Elements

Whether you realize it or not, we all treat mealtime as a ritual. In a very natural way, you pick up your child, put him in his high chair, put on his bib, and pick up a bowl and spoon. These elements—high chair, bib, bowl and spoon—are constant for the child while he eats and thus enable him to develop the habit. Repeating this association of external elements along with the ritual (in this case, eating) gives the child a feeling of security. After a while, he becomes so familiar with the whole process that as soon as he sees the bowl, he waves his little arms in anticipation of the meal to come.

EXTERNAL ELEMENTS
ASSOCIATED WITH A HABIT

- External elements associated with eating include plates, cups, spoons, bibs, and so on.

- Use these elements only during the activity of eating.

- Take these elements away when the activity is completed.

Exhibition of a Confident Attitude

Keep in mind that kids always pick up adults' moods and emotions. From the very first days of life, a baby understands what you are communicating through your tone; he doesn't have to know the meaning of the words to know if you are angry or happy.

So it doesn't matter if you call him "chubby" or "brat" as long you say it in a sweet voice. On the other hand, a child will surely freak out when he hears "You are so handsome, my darling," if you say it like the child in *The Exorcist*.

In just the same way, your child can sense your confidence or hesitation as you go through your daily activities. If his caretakers seem unsure of how to feed him, bathe him, dress him, or put him to sleep, then he'll feel insecure at these times, too.

When confident and relaxed parents teach their child to eat, the child notices this and feels confident and relaxed as well.

Parents don't let their kids alter the eating habits they have taught them. If your child sticks his hand into the bowl or sprays orange juice out of his mouth, you will explain to him that he is acting incorrectly. Then you will show him the right way to behave.

Nobody would think that a child would be traumatized by being "forced" to eat yogurt with a spoon, right? After all, when you explain this to your child, you do it in a deliberate and natural way, not as if you are punishing him. Nobody

would say, "You've been bad, and now you have to eat your soup with a spoon." If you don't transmit a feeling of punishment, he won't ever feel threatened by the event.

Sleeping is different. Parents frequently punish their children by making them go to bed. And in doing so they make their children associate "bed" with punishment—with something negative and even traumatic.

What Happens if You Express Insecurity While Putting Your Child to Bed?

Let's imagine, for a moment, a situation in which parents abandon accepted mealtime elements such as the high chair, bib, bowl, and spoon. Let's imagine that, instead, they exchange the bib for an embroidered silk shawl and the bowl for a motorcycle helmet, and instead of putting the child in a high chair they decide to set him up in the basketball net in the backyard while they try to score baskets with spoonfuls of baby food from the dining room window.

Absurd, right? Well, now think about what you have been willing to do when your kid starts bawling at midnight. You stand on your head, do the hokey pokey, imitate Barney, or try to hypnotize your child by swaying the hanging lamp in front of his little face. What is the poor kid going to think? He'll probably want to grow up as quickly as possible so that he can sue you.

Seriously, with so much doubt and improvisation, parents are transmitting insecurity. Your child picks up on the fact that you feel overwhelmed, don't know what to do, and are making it up as you go along. He won't learn how to get himself to sleep until you show him how confident you are that he can do it on his own.

HOW DO CHILDREN COMMUNICATE?

Kids are clever little people. From the moment they're born, they observe their parents carefully. They know how to act in order to get you to respond to their desires and demands; which is to say, they know perfectly well that every *action* on their part provokes a *reaction* from you. As the baby grows, so does his ability to communicate with adults.

HOW DO CHILDREN COMMUNICATE?

Through the action–reaction principle. Therefore:

• Adults should ignore inappropriate behavior.

• Adults should reinforce appropriate behavior.

Let's look at a breakdown of your child's communication development.

From Six to Eighteen Months (Pre-Speech Children)

During this stage of development, children communicate with their parents by doing something that causes a reaction. At this stage they can:

• Smile, say "goo goo gaa gaa," clap, and the like. With these cute tricks, they get their parents all excited and puffed up with pride. Still, after the twentieth "goo goo," you've probably stopped listening.

• Cry, scream, vomit, hit themselves, et cetera. With this effective repertoire, kids get your full attention. You come running to their side. There is, of course, nothing really wrong with them; they are just trying to attract attention and have some company.

In other words, when a child doesn't know how to fall asleep by himself and feels insecure, he will try with all his might to get your attention. Once he has seen that no one comes running from mere gurgling, he will use other, more dramatic devices. This may alarm you—and for good reason!—but don't let it frighten you. It's very easy for a child to make himself vomit, but he'll never go so far as to actually hurt himself. I promise that he will give up once he understands that you aren't impressed.

From Eighteen Months to Five Years Old

At this age, children acquire the weapon of language. However, they use it in a different way than adults do. For a three-year-old, speaking is just another method of making people respond. Children know that when they say certain words, their parents will react immediately. After much trial and error, they know that:

- A "Mama-Coca-Cola" at two in the morning doesn't work at all.

- A "Daddy-thirsty" repeated twenty times at two in the morning gets Daddy out of bed on the twenty-first. Your child will drink it even if he isn't thirsty just so you'll think, *Aww, poor kid, he was really thirsty.* Now he's got you.

- A "Mommy-tummy-hurts" works every time. Every mother will rush to her child's side to make sure he's okay.

In conclusion, in order to get your attention, your child will use the most shocking and effective words, even if they have

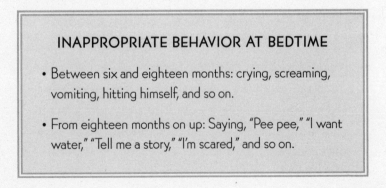

INAPPROPRIATE BEHAVIOR AT BEDTIME

- Between six and eighteen months: crying, screaming, vomiting, hitting himself, and so on.

- From eighteen months on up: Saying, "Pee pee," "I want water," "Tell me a story," "I'm scared," and so on.

no basis in reality, and even if he doesn't know exactly what they mean.

Dealing with Inappropriate Bedtime Behavior

Your child's tantrums and desperate attempts to get your attention are inappropriate. There are two possibilities for dealing with this type of behavior.

1. Ignore the behavior.

2. Answer these cries for attention.

Let's look at a simple example. Your child wants you to give him something in his room. But rather than asking for it directly, he points and starts to bawl. Bawling, in this case, is the inappropriate behavior. You can deal with this by:

- Ignoring his shrieks, pretending not to listen, and not giving him what he wants. This will teach him that he shouldn't ask for things by crying his eyes out. He'll learn that he needs to find another way.

- Giving him what he wants because his shrill screams are driving you crazy and shattering the glass cabinets. If you respond to your child's demands in this way, he will think that it's normal. You will be *reinforcing* this inappropriate behavior.

Your child will continue or discontinue behaviors based on your reaction. When he learns that he gets what he wants by crying, it becomes a learned behavior. The more you reinforce it, the more difficult it will be for your child to learn to act appropriately.

So the best thing to do is to modify inappropriate behavior as soon as possible. The approach is the same for a child of eight months or for a four-year-old. *Always ignore inappropriate behavior!*

SUMMARY

Learning Good Sleep Habits
How can you instill a habit in your child?

- By associating and maintaining constant external elements. At feeding time, for example, you always use the same high chair, bib, bowl and spoon.

- By expressing confidence while showing your child appropriate behavior.

How do children communicate?

By doing things that make adults react. Children between six and eighteen months (pre-speech children) get their parents to react by:

- Smiling, saying "goo goo gaa gaa," clapping, and the like.

- Crying, screaming, vomiting, hitting themselves, et cetera.

Children between eighteen months and five years of age get their parents to react by:

- Using words to get attention—for example, "Mommy-tummy-hurts." Sometimes they will even use words they don't understand that achieve the desired reaction.

As parents, you should ignore your child's inappropriate behavior. Instead of reinforcing this behavior, teach him appropriate ways to act.

Chapter 3

How to Teach Good Sleep Habits

Now I'm going to show you how to apply the theory you have learned so far to the problem of bedtime. Remember that the method is the same whether your child is nine months or four and a half years old. Let's start with a clean slate. What you have previously done to get your child to sleep is neither right nor wrong, but let's put it aside for now.

PREPARE THE TEACHING MATERIALS

First of all, you need to choose the right external elements.

Just as your child associates a bowl and a spoon with eating, she'll soon associate the elements you have chosen with sleeping. Soon, very soon, these elements will become essential for falling asleep; she'll also need them every time she wakes up during the night. Nighttime wakings are part of a normal sleep pattern even though we don't remember them the next day. Therefore, it is very important that you don't become one of these elements. *You, the parent, should not play an essential role in helping your child fall asleep.* This means that you have to disappear from the room before your child has fallen asleep. Don't help her fall asleep by rocking her, giving her a massage, or cuddling her. If you do this, she'll demand your presence every time she wakes up and you might as well invest in a comfy armchair, where you will spend every night for the rest of her childhood.

For your child to learn to sleep without your help, you must stop:

- Singing to her.

- Cradling her in your arms.

- Rocking her in her crib.

- Holding her hand.

- Pushing her around in a stroller.

- Driving her around in the car.

- Touching her or letting her touch your hair.

- Caressing her or patting her back.

- Giving her a bottle or nursing her to calm her down.

- Putting her in your bed.

- Letting her run around until she tires herself out.

- Giving her water simply because she cries for it.

It's all a matter of association. If, for example, you are holding her hand when she goes to sleep, when she wakes up, she will expect you to still be holding her hand. This will not only frighten her but also prompt her to ask for your hand in order to go back to sleep. To put this in perspective, imagine that you go to sleep with your partner . . . but when you wake up, your partner isn't there anymore. It'll be pretty tough to get back to sleep, right?

Instead of giving your child your presence, you need to provide the objects and conditions that will keep her company throughout the night. That way, if she suddenly wakes up, she will have what she needs to put herself back to sleep.

It's your responsibility to choose these elements, but here are some suggestions:

- Find a stuffed animal that will always sleep with your child. It can be one you already have, or you can buy a new one. Once you've decided on one, give it a name. Let's call our stuffed animal Mr. Cuddle.

- If your child uses a pacifier, it's a good idea to spread a few around on her mattress so that if she wakes up in the middle of the night, it will be easy for her to find one and put it in her mouth.

APPROPRIATE ELEMENTS ASSOCIATED WITH SLEEP

- Stuffed animals.

- Pacifiers (if they use them already).

- Mobile/wall decoration.

- Foot pajamas.

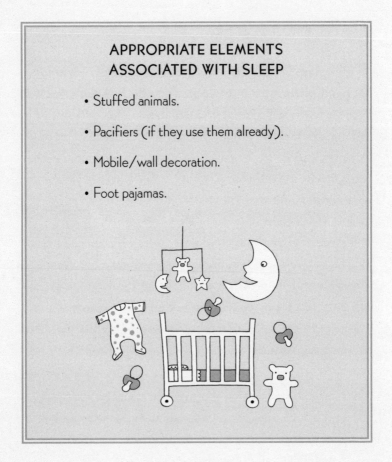

• Use external elements—mobiles, wall decorations—
for your child to see when she opens her eyes. For
example, paste a cutout moon on the wall or hang a
mobile to keep your child company every night. Place
this at a safe distance so that she can't touch it and
doesn't try to grab it.

• By six months, your kid will move in her sleep and
will probably kick off the covers. I recommend putting
her to bed with foot pajamas so she'll stay warm and
you won't have to worry about endlessly getting up to
tuck her in.

GETTING UNDER WAY

Research has proven that children fall asleep more easily between the hours of 7 and 8 PM. Use this as a guideline for es-
tablishing your own schedule. Once you have set your
routine, stick to it!

The sleep schedule you create determines the timing for
other activities. For example, if your baby goes to bed at
7:30 PM, then she should eat dinner at around 6:30 PM. (Remember that meals help us "wind the clock.") And if you usually bathe her in the evening, then a good time is just before
dinner.

When your child has finished eating, take away all the elements associated with the activity, including the glass of milk

or juice. By doing this, you'll help her understand that there is a particular time for eating, and she won't use the excuse of "I'm hungry" or "I'm thirsty" when she feels alone and insecure in her room. You want to reinforce that there is a time and place for each activity.

MENTALLY PREPARE THE "PROFESSOR"

Adopt a firm and confident attitude.

As I explained earlier when analyzing eating habits, your child needs to feel that you know what you are doing and why you are doing it.

Now you know that there is a scientific approach for teaching your child how to sleep. From here on out, just concentrate on following the method as I lay it out here and don't

REMEMBER

- You are the teacher.

- Your child is the student.

- You must be convinced of your success in order to begin.

- You must not alter any of the guidelines.

- If you let your child win just once, the method will fail.

Recommended Routines Beginning at Six Months of Age

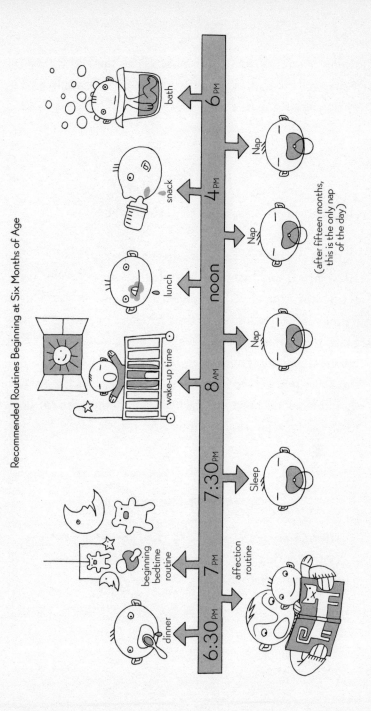

(after fifteen months, this is the only nap of the day)

alter it because of your child's antics. This method will be effective only if your follow it to a T and show complete conviction as you use it.

STEP BY STEP

Here are some more specific tools you can use.

Before Bed: The Affection Routine

After dinner and bath time, spend five to ten minutes interacting with your child in a relaxed and enjoyable way. This is a time for reading a story, singing a lullaby, or playing a quiet game. It is a time for kisses, laughing, and cuddles. I don't recommend watching television, playing video games, or anything else that gets your child too worked up. Such activities should never take place in the bedroom. Remember, the bedroom is for sleeping and nothing else.

THE AFFECTION ROUTINE

Once dinner is over, you should spend five to ten minutes with your child. This is a time for you to clearly demonstrate your affection.

During this time, show your child how much you love her. Sleep is not a punishment.

In the Room

Once you've finished the affection routine, carry your child to her bedroom, where the ingredients you have prepared will be waiting for her: Mr. Cuddle, the mobile, and the pacifiers (if she uses them).

So what should you do next?

No matter what your child is doing—and she will try everything under the sun—concentrate on the following process.

Lay the child down in her bed or crib. If she gets up, cries, or objects, don't lose your cool. She *will* get confused by any change in your attitude. Next, hold her hand for a few brief moments. Slowly, but not glacially, move a few feet away from her. Then, in a calm, sweet, but firm tone of voice, say:

> *"Sweetie, Mommy/Daddy is going to teach you how to sleep all by yourself. Starting today, you are going to sleep here, in your crib, with your poster of the moon, your mobile, and Mr. Cuddle."*

Repeat this speech. The importance of these words lies in your assured tone of voice. Once again, the key is a confident attitude.

IN THE ROOM

- Use a calm, soft voice that communicates *confidence*.

- Speak to your child for thirty seconds, explaining that you are teaching her how to sleep alone.

- Repeat the monologue until thirty seconds is up. This is not a dialogue, so you shouldn't respond to any questions or react to any of her behaviors at this time.

What Will Your Child Do?

Your child is extremely clever and creative and will try every trick in the book to break down your confidence.

It's very likely that while you are giving your short speech, your child will intuit what is to come and throw a tantrum. Don't change your tone of voice or stop speaking. Don't enter into a conversation. Essentially, you need to become deaf and blind during this stage.

This is the moment in which you will suffer the most. Remember what I said earlier: Your child is extremely intelligent and knows how to come up with viable objections and to act in ways that will tug at your heartstrings. I called this "inappropriate behavior," and it's your job to correct it. Since your child can't read this book, she doesn't know what is happen-

ing. The burden is on you to do all of the work. So pluck up your courage, turn off the light, and leave the room.

Once the Light Is Turned Off

After you've made your short speech, leave the room. From this moment on, you will need nerves of steel. I'll be honest. The first two nights of the treatment are rough. The best way to get through them is to run this mantra through your head: *By the fifth night, my child will have magically transformed into a wonderful little bedbug.*

Still, until this charm works, you must follow the procedure with the confidence of a saint. When your child keeps crying and won't calm down, wait exactly one minute, then enter her room to comfort her. After all, she's not going to learn good sleep habits without your help. Think back to when you learned to ski or swim. You always had someone keeping an eye on you, right? It's the same thing here: Keep an eye on her while, at the same time, enabling her to fall asleep on her own. So instead of ordering that comfy armchair and giving up a good night's sleep for the next few years, I recommend making a few short visits to her bedroom to calm her down.

- Do not go into her room to help her go to sleep.

- Go into her room only to show her that you haven't abandoned her.

During these visits, don't do anything except repeat the short monologue I quoted earlier, lightly placing your hand on your child. Do not kiss her, rock her, or hold her hand. Remind her in a calm, serene tone that you are teaching her to sleep. At all costs, avoid making her feel scolded, punished, or abandoned. Remember that when you go into her bedroom, it is not to quiet her down, but rather to affectionately show her that you will always be there for her.

How Often Should You Make the Visits?

If your child keeps screaming and crying, which she probably will, go back into her room after three minutes have passed. This is the second visit. If the situation doesn't improve, you should wait another five minutes before making your third visit. Each visit should be identical. Recite the speech and then leave. Never start a conversation with your child or pay attention to her protests. As you now know, she is acting out in order to get a reaction. There's no reason to be scared or to cave, not even if she vomits or bangs her head against her crib. It sounds harsh, of course, but if you keep this up without any exceptions, your child will be sleeping through the night in just a few short days. And so will you. And maybe even your neighbors!

If you don't lose your patience, your little one will be sleeping better in less than one week. Just continue to give your speech with a sweet, calm, but firm attitude no matter what time of the night it may be. You'll see. It's not that hard. If you are positive and confident, your child will understand your loving intentions.

Take a look at table 1, which details the intervals of time that you should wait between one visit and the next. Make adjustments if you must, but always follow a progression (see table 2). Far more important than the exact number of minutes that you leave between visits is a calm and confident performance each time you go in. By repeating a phrase such as,

TABLE 1

NIGHTLY VISIT SCHEDULE

Day	1st Waiting Period	2nd Waiting Period	3rd and Subsequent Waiting Periods
1	1 minute	3 minutes	5 minutes
2	2 minutes	5 minutes	8 minutes
3	3 minutes	7 minutes	11 minutes
4	4 minutes	9 minutes	14 minutes
5	5 minutes	11 minutes	17 minutes
Following days			
6	6 minutes	13 minutes	20 minutes
7	7 minutes	15 minutes	23 minutes

Continue this progression until your child is sleeping on her own.

TABLE 2

NIGHTLY VISIT SCHEDULE: SAMPLE ADJUSTMENT

Day	1st Waiting Period	2nd Waiting Period	3rd and Subsequent Waiting Periods
1	1 minute	2 minutes	3 minutes
2	2 minutes	3 minutes	4 minutes
3	3 minutes	4 minutes	5 minutes
4	4 minutes	5 minutes	6 minutes
5	5 minutes	6 minutes	7 minutes
6	6 minutes	7 minutes	8 minutes

"Your Mommy/Daddy loves you very much and that is why I'm teaching you to sleep," you communicate confidence.

If you follow this method, you child *will* sleep. Sooner or later, after much crying and many frustrated attempts, she'll see that she doesn't have any other option. She'll know that you haven't abandoned her, but she'll also understand that you won't be manipulated by her many tricks.

Until she learns to fall asleep on her own, however, it is very likely that she'll wake up again during the night and request your presence by crying. If in the past she was used to falling asleep with you in the room, she will probably miss this and start to cry. From now on, you won't be there—but Mr. Cuddle will. When your child wakes up during the night, just repeat the visits at the proper time intervals and recite the monologue that you know so well. Muster up all the serenity you've got, even if it's 5 AM. Finally, remember not to show any hint of anger or frustration, at least not while you are in the room. You can do it! Just take a deep breath and stay in control.

- Your child doesn't have a watch, so she doesn't know what time it is.

- Each and every time she wakes up, follow the timetable and the method.

- Follow these same guidelines at nap times.

SUMMARY

How to Teach Good Sleep Habits

Teaching a child to sleep should be done in exactly the same way for a baby as for a four-year-old. To start with, follow these three steps:

1. *Prepare the external elements.* Choose the elements that will accompany your child throughout the night: a stuffed animal (Mr. Cuddle), a few pacifiers (if she uses them), a mobile/wall decoration (out of reach), and/or foot pajamas.

2. *Establish a schedule.* Use meals and baths to cue bedtime.

3. *Prepare yourself mentally.* Adopt a firm, confident attitude.

Step by Step

- *The affection routine.* After bath time and dinnertime, spend five to ten minutes with your child doing something you both enjoy.

- *Bedtime.* Put your child in her bed and repeat the monologue, "Sweetie, Mommy/Daddy is going to teach you how to sleep all by yourself. Starting today you are going to sleep here, in your crib, with the poster of the moon, the mobile, and Mr. Cuddle." Then leave the room.

• *Visits*. If your child cries inconsolably, make short visits to calm her down, but not to put her to sleep. Maintain fixed intervals between each of the visits.

Chapter 4

Questions and Concerns

work long hours every day. At night, I'm exhausted, and I'm not sure that I'll be able to stay calm if I start following the method under these conditions. Would it be better to wait until I have some time off to begin treatment? When is the best time to start?

The adage *Never put off till tomorrow what you can do today* applies here. Your child needs to start sleeping well as soon as possible, and so do you. Don't postpone treatment any longer! As soon as you have finished reading these pages, you can begin. Here are four important points to keep in mind before you start:

1. *Be convinced that it works*. Confidence! My method has proven to work in 96 percent of cases, which isn't a bad track record. Having this self-assurance will keep

you from losing control. Remind yourself that by teaching your child to sleep well, you are helping him to be healthier and happier. It would never occur to you to say that you're too exhausted to feed your child, right? Teaching him to sleep well is just as important as making sure he eats.

2. *Understand how the method works*. Read this book carefully before you begin, and consult your pediatrician if you have any questions.

3. *Start when your family routine is stable*. Start using this method during a normal week. Avoid starting during a vacation, when you are in the middle of moving, or when you are entertaining visitors. All these factors can negatively affect how you carry out the method. Before you begin, make sure that there are no expected circumstances that are likely to disrupt normal family life in the following ten days.

4. *Make sure your child is healthy*. If he becomes sick in the middle of treatment, go in and console him every time he cries, and follow your pediatrician's advice. Take your child's temperature; give him his prescribed medicine and water, if he wants it. While you are tending to him, be affectionate and sweet, but not lenient. After all, if you change the routine while he is sick, it will be harder later to go back to the method. Teething

may also cause your child to cry, but should not inter-
fere with the treatment.

*I'm in the habit of reading in bed, and I usually fall asleep with the
bedside table lamp still on. My four-year-old son says that he is
afraid of the dark and complains if I turn off his lamp—and he
notes that I always sleep with mine on. Should I buy a night-light
for his room?*

Except in rare cases, kids with insomnia are not afraid of the
dark. What these kids are afraid of is sleep itself. It is true,
however, that darkness creates a scary environment in which
a kid's normal daytime fantasies can turn into terrifying mon-
sters. So if your child isn't particularly fearful during the day,
don't worry too much about nighttime fears; go ahead and
turn the light off.

Fear turns out to be one of the most effective excuses for a
child to get his parent's attention. This is understandable.
Few things move an adult more than seeing a child suffer. But
in most cases, he's just using this to get your attention. Don't
place too much importance on it; consider it another inappropriate behavior to be ignored.

Finally, light should never be associated with sleep. If you
let your child do so, he will expect the light to be on when he
wakes up in the middle of the night, and when it isn't he will
feel frightened. So rule out night-lights and any toys that
glow in the dark. Oh, and if you are accustomed to falling
asleep with the light on, try improving your own sleep habits

by turning it off before you fall asleep. After all, it would set a good example for your child.

My son is eleven months old and has a tendency to throw up at the slightest unpleasant thing. What should I do if he throws up when I'm teaching him how to sleep? Should I interrupt the method and start again the next day?

As I explained before, vomiting is very easy for a baby to do and has no major consequences aside from an extremely strong reaction in all parents. So again, my response is to consider it inappropriate behavior and ignore it. What's most important is to continue following the method; at the end, you will have a child who not only sleeps well but doesn't throw up all the time. When your child vomits, limit your response to cleaning him up without getting upset or punishing him. Then, no matter what time it is, repeat your well-used monologue. Soon your baby will learn that acting out doesn't get attention.

I used your method at home and got my son to sleep well in just five days. Now we are about to leave for a vacation, and I'm afraid that all my work will be ruined. What measures should I take while we are away?

It's not necessary for you to try to bring your child's entire room with you on vacation. But you absolutely shouldn't forget Mr. Cuddle and the pacifiers (if he uses them). If your child is old enough to understand a simple conversation, explain to him that he will sleep in a different bed on vacation and that when you return he will go back to sleeping in his own bedroom.

Four months ago, we adopted a three-year-old girl from Nepal. During the day she behaves well, but at night she doesn't sleep and always climbs into our bed for reassurance and affection. We want to follow your method, but we are afraid that she may feel abandoned if we leave her alone in her room. Her English is shaky and we are afraid that she won't understand when we repeat the monologue.

In the case of an adopted child who has experienced abandonment, decide before beginning the method if it is more important for you to teach her good sleep habits or to establish a strong emotional bond with her for another few weeks. You are the ones who know the child best, so you will know what she needs most. For more information, contact your pediatrician.

Although each child has unique needs, after a month or so your newly adopted child will most likely have accepted you as her family and will be ready to learn to sleep. If you do decide to start using the method during this early transitional stage, don't hesitate to let some things slide. Still, while you are adapting the method to your child's needs, remember that you do not want to reward inappropriate behaviors; nor do you want to be an essential element in her sleep process. You just want to provide love, affection, and the support she needs to be able to learn to sleep on her own.

Don't worry about the language issue. As I explained earlier, kids pick up on your tone of voice and don't need to understand the words in order to know what you are trying to get across. When you repeat the monologue to your adopted child in a sweet and loving tone, she will understand what you are saying as well as any child born into an English-speaking family.

When my husband and I go away for the weekend, we usually leave our daughter with my in-laws. They spoil her rotten and don't use your sleep method. How can we make them understand that it is essential for them to follow your guidelines at bedtime?

As we all know, parents educate their children, and grandparents spoil them. While I am not against pampering, it can undermine the treatment, especially at the beginning. For this reason, I advise against letting your child sleep at her grandparents' house at the start. Give yourselves and your daughter at least ten days to adjust to the new sleep routines. Then, once your daughter is used to sleeping well, you can send her off for a weekend with her grandparents.

At this point, the initial phase is over and others can put her to bed without being overwhelmed with instructions. They'll do what they want to anyway, so just explain the importance of her bedtime schedules and who Mr. Cuddle is. Your child will soon understand that staying with Grandma and Grandpa is an exception to the sleep routine that she follows at home, which gives her a sense of security no matter where she goes to sleep. On the other hand, if for any reason your child has to sleep at her grandparents' house for a significant amount of time, they should be "trained" to follow the method just as you do.

I want to start following the method as soon as possible, but right now my son spends eight hours in day care and takes his nap there. Should I talk with the day care center?

The caretakers at day care centers are excellent professionals trained to treat all children equally. They have very set routines and schedules, and, as a result, children feel secure and generally nap well. Instead of trying to talk to these professionals, concentrate on creating and maintaining good sleep habits at home. By doing this, your child will develop a strong sense of security toward sleep both at home and afar.

My wife and I separated six months ago and now I only see my four-year-old son every fifteen days. When he visits, we usually play in bed, and he always falls asleep with me. My wife recently told me I shouldn't do this because she has started to follow your method. It is really so bad if I put him to bed this way?

Yes, it is. It's completely understandable that you enjoy this time with him, but at this point, it is more important for your child to sleep well than for you to have an extra fifteen minutes with him. In addition, as parents you should always work together to educate your child even though you are separated. When your son comes to spend the weekend with you, help him understand that you will be together all day long, but that at night he will go to sleep in his own bed with all the external elements he has at home with Mommy.

My two-year-old daughter has Down syndrome. Do you think I should adapt the guidelines and consult a pediatrician before starting to follow your method?

Children with Down syndrome or any type of mental disability can learn to sleep just like any other child by following the same treatment. It may be somewhat more difficult to teach them since they usually have a shorter attention span, but never underestimate their ability to understand you.

Children with special needs learn according to the same principle of action and reaction as other kids: Treat her as you would any other child. As you know, the temperament of Down syndrome children is very particular. They are especially sensitive and affectionate, which affects your way of interacting with them. However, remember never to confuse caring and sweetness with overprotection and leniency. Stick to the guidelines and I can assure you that your little girl will sleep properly.

And yes, it is a good idea for parents of children with special needs to consult a child psychologist or psychiatrist to determine if they need any therapeutic help.

We recently moved into a duplex with bedrooms on the second floor. A few weeks ago, our son climbed out of his crib, and now we are afraid that one day he may fall down the stairs. What should we do?

Things get much more complicated when your child is old enough to be able to get out of his crib. But if he starts to do this, don't shut the door to his room. A closed door only upsets children and makes them feel that they are being punished—which, as I've discussed, is a bad bedtime association. Instead, I recommend installing a small gate in the doorway to prevent him from getting out of the room. These are not hard to find in specialty stores, or you can have one tailor-made.

As always, interact with him in a calm and confident way and don't let yourself get tricked into making changes to the method. If your child falls asleep on the floor, just pick him up and gently carry him back to his bed. If he wakes up in your arms, simply put him back under the covers and continue following the set guidelines you know so well by now.

My son is four and a half years old, and although he has never slept well, I think he will figure it out soon enough. Is it worth it for me to start using the method?

Of course it is. If your child doesn't learn how to sleep correctly before he is five years old and no one solves his infantile insomnia, he will end up suffering from what is clinically called *learned insomnia*. The symptoms of this type of problem are:

- Showing fear of sleep and the dark.

- Postponing bedtime for as long as possible.

- Making excuses to sleep with the parents.

- Refusing to sleep in other houses or at summer camp.

- Feeling restless as bedtime approaches.

- Considering bedtime an unpleasant activity.

- Sleeping too few hours.

The consequences of learned insomnia affect the entire family, but above all they affect the child, who can suffer on physical, psychological, and academic levels. What's more, teaching good sleep habits is more difficult once children reach the age of five. Not only are these children more resourceful and less willing to change ingrained behavior, but they are also much more adept at using emotional blackmail that can make even the most seasoned parent lose heart. So don't dally another minute! I assure you, it's worth it.

Our oldest son never had any problems with sleeping, and he quickly made the transition from his crib to his bed. Our youngest child, however, doesn't want to sleep in her own bed. She's three years old now and always comes into ours. When should she learn to sleep in her own bed?

A baby's first weeks of life are a really crazy time for the entire family. At that point, it is very normal for your child to sleep in your bedroom—it's easier and quicker to feed her and take care of her needs there. By the time she is three months old, however, she should be able to sleep in her own room, though it is still quite normal for her to stay with her mother up to six months of age to make nighttime feeding easier.

The switch from crib to bed should be made when your child is too big for the crib and when her behavior indicates that she's ready (she can stand up and climb out of the crib). This switch should always be made at a good time for your child and should be postponed if there are special circumstances, such as the arrival of a new sibling, the beginning of kindergarten, or a move from one house to another. Don't forget to congratulate your child for being "a big girl" and for having "such a pretty bed" that you are sure she will sleep well in.

I'm afraid that there is no solution for my son's insomnia. I've tried the method three times at home and haven't been able to teach him to sleep. What's wrong?

It's true that in some cases the method works better than in others, but don't lose hope. Let's go over what may be giving you problems. Try to be honest with yourself when answering the following questions.

First, are you sure that you've followed the method correctly? Remember, never bend the rules. Parents frequently make adaptations of the method, and this hardly ever works.

Do all the child's caretakers fully understand the method and agree to follow it? If one parent but not the other follows the rules, for instance, they are sure to fail. If your child is put to bed often by other caretakers (babysitter, grandparents, and other family members), are those caretakers trained to use the method?

Finally, are you having difficulty following the method? Even when you understand it, there are sometimes reasons why you can't follow through with it. There may be difficulties with the child:

- He has gotten sick and is on medication. (In this case, wait until he gets better.)

- He has a developmental problem. (Contact your pediatrician, who can advise you on what to do.)

- He has an irritable disposition. (Consult a child psychologist or psychiatrist to decide what to do.)

There may also be problems with the parent. Insecurity is very common. Sometimes it just isn't easy to admit that you've been unable to carry out appropriate routines because of an emotional, psychological, or sociocultural problem. Pronounced insecurity makes a parent especially vulnerable. (See page 23, where I explain how a child picks up on his parent's nonverbal communication.)

It's possible that emotional or psychopathological disorders are involved. The most frequent ones are:

- Family stress.

- Maternal or paternal depression.

- Maternal or paternal pathological rejection of the child.

- Conflicting feelings on the part of a parent.

These types of situations usually cause:

- Sudden changes in attitude.

- Feelings of guilt.

- Overstimulation of the child.

- Periods of unconsciously ignoring the child.

- Difficulties maintaining balanced behavior.

- Difficulties creating appropriate habits.

Other secondary emotional disturbances include:

- Difficulties with feeding. Poor sleeping and eating habits often go together; the main cause is a lack of confidence.

- Increase in anxiety due to a specific family problem.

- Marital problems between the parents.

Here are some solutions to these problems:

- Recognize the problems you are facing and try to get over the situation by rereading the method carefully, discussing it with your partner or other caretakers, and designating the person who can best follow the method as the one who uses it the most.

- If you think that you can't solve the problem by yourself, seek the help of a psychologist or psychiatrist.

Once my son has learned to sleep correctly, is it possible that he will have sleep problems again?

In general, no. The method is remarkably effective. After all, when someone has learned to eat correctly, he doesn't question whether all of a sudden he will one day forget how to do it. It's the same with sleep. However, it is true that in some rare cases (such as following a psychological trauma or illness) there can be a regression. If this happens, start the treatment again from the beginning. But don't worry too much. You will have already begun to communicate true confidence and will understand why this attitude is essential for enabling your child to sleep correctly.

Chapter 5

Recent Research:
How to Teach Your Child
to Sleep Well from Day One

From the moment a child is born, there is already an established pattern of sleep and wakefulness. He'll wake up approximately every three to four hours, needing to eat, have his diaper changed, and hear your voice. This kind of exchange is very important while he is awake.

I have already established that an infant follows sleep patterns very similar to those of a fetus. He experiences what I call *active sleep:* His eyes move; his chin quivers; he may breathe irregularly, sigh, and move his extremities. This type of sleep, even while it may seem restless, is completely normal and should never be interrupted.

After thirty to forty minutes of this sleep phase (active sleep), the infant enters into a deeper sleep called *restful sleep.* In this stage, he is completely relaxed, he doesn't sigh or move, and he breathes softly and deeply. This stage lasts for another thirty to forty minutes.

Your child will alternate between these two sleep phases

until he wakes up after three to four hours. This sleep pattern lasts until the infant is two months old.

RECOMMENDATIONS FOR CREATING GOOD SLEEP HABITS

After each feeding (whether breast or bottle—whichever you have decided on), keep your child awake in your arms for around fifteen minutes. It is very important for your child to be awake while he eats so that he learns to associate food with wakefulness. This also improves the elimination of gases and can possibly avoid colic. After changing his diaper, lovingly put him in his crib so that he learns to go to sleep on his own.

A word of advice: Never forget that your baby picks up on all the sensations that you (his parent) transmit. If you are re-laxed and speak to him sweetly, he will feel this and respond in kind. On the other hand, if you express nervousness or change his routines continuously, your baby will become nervous as well.

When possible, I highly recommend that you feed your baby in a consistent location, in a stable and comfortable temperature, with a light on and soft music playing. Your baby should be awake during these feedings. This may seem difficult since he will tend to fall asleep as he nurses or bottle-feeds. Therefore, you should speak, caress him, and find other loving ways to keep him awake. As I said before, this helps to teach him to associate eating with being awake.

You should also know about two important instinctual reflexes in infants. All babies are born with innate reflexes. The two most developed of these at birth are the sucking reflex and the monkey reflex. The latter is characterized by the movement an infant makes when he hears a noise or when you move him: He stretches his arms out, simulating a hug. This is completely normal. You can experiment with it by clapping softly near your child and watching how he reacts.

What is more important for parents to know about, however, is the sucking reflex. All infants will suck on whatever is put in their mouths. This reflex logically helps them eat, but they will do it at any given moment, not only when they are hungry. You can test this by putting your index finger (after cleaning it, of course) near your baby's mouth. He will search for the finger and suck it softly, even if he has just eaten.

Many people falsely think that an infant is hungry when he puts his hand in his mouth and sucks it. All that the baby is doing is acting on his sucking reflex. If this is misinterpreted, you might have a tendency to feed your infant at inappropriate times or—worse—too frequently. By doing this, you run the risk of instilling bad habits.

During his first month of life, an infant usually feeds six to seven times over the course of twenty-four hours. The pediatrician is, of course, the one who should determine if the infant is receiving enough nutrition for appropriate growth. All children are different, but they all follow more or less similar patterns. Infants who breast-feed, which is still considered the most appropriate food for infants nutritionally, may feed slightly but not significantly more frequently.

After his first month of life, an infant usually only feeds five times a day, since he is beginning to increase his consecutive hours of sleep during the night. If the mother maintains a flexible but primarily fixed routine, the infant will develop feeding patterns that resemble breakfast, lunch, snack, dinner, and a night feeding.

At around three months, an infant's nightly sleep period is defined and consists of around six hours of sleep. The daily feedings continue at a frequency of approximately four hours, followed by naps. Some infants may enter into a nightly sleep pattern earlier, and this is also quite normal.

At six months, an infant's sleep cycle is quite set. It consists of four daily feedings followed by a short nap after the

breakfast feeding, a longer nap (around three hours) after the lunch feeding, and another short nap (at least an hour) after the snack-time feeding. Finally, after having his bath, an evening feeding, and a story or song, he will begin his nightly sleeping period of twelve hours.

SUMMARY

My main intention in this book is to help your baby develop the ability to fall asleep on his own, without the presence of a parent.

Techniques for Teaching your Child to Sleep Well Starting from Day 1

- When it is possible, I highly recommend that you feed your baby in the same place, in a comfortable and consistent temperature, with a light on and soft music playing. Your baby should be awake during these feedings so that he learns to associate eating with being awake.

- After each feeding, keep your baby awake in your arms for around fifteen minutes. This improves the elimination of gases, may reduce the chance of colic, and helps to begin digestion.

- After changing his diaper, it is important to lovingly put your baby in his crib so that he learns how to go to sleep on his own. You can use a pacifier or a stuffed animal to aid in the process. If the pacifier falls out of his mouth, patiently teach him to put it back in by himself.

- Follow this schedule for your baby's daily feedings. At night, you can feed him in your bed, but after changing his diaper (if it is necessary) you should put him back in his crib while he is still awake.

- It's very important for mothers to follow the same routines as the infant. This is a way of avoiding postpartum depression. It has been proven that one of the factors leading to postpartum depression is the lack of sleep so many mothers experience while feeding their babies.

ACKNOWLEDGMENTS

Magdalena Bandera,
writer

Montse Domènech,
psychologist and teacher

Montse Santamarina,
writer

Rosa Caballero,
child psychiatrist

About the Author

EDUARD ESTIVILL, M.D., is director of the Sleep
Disturbances Clinic at the Institut Dexeus in Barcelona,
Spain, where he is also head of the Neurophysiology Unit.
Trained in both America and Spain, he is a specialist in
pediatrics, neurophysiology, and sleep medicine.

About the Type

This book was set in Goudy, a typeface designed by Frederic William Goudy (1865–1947). Goudy began his career as a bookkeeper, but devoted the rest of his life to the pursuit of "recognized quality" in a printing type.
Goudy was produced in 1914 and was an instant bestseller for the foundry. It has generous curves and smooth, even color. It is regarded as one of Goudy's finest achievements.